Success
Assessment Papers

English
10 – 11 years · levels 4 – 5

Alison Head

clear instructional text

level showing attainment target

paper number for quick reference

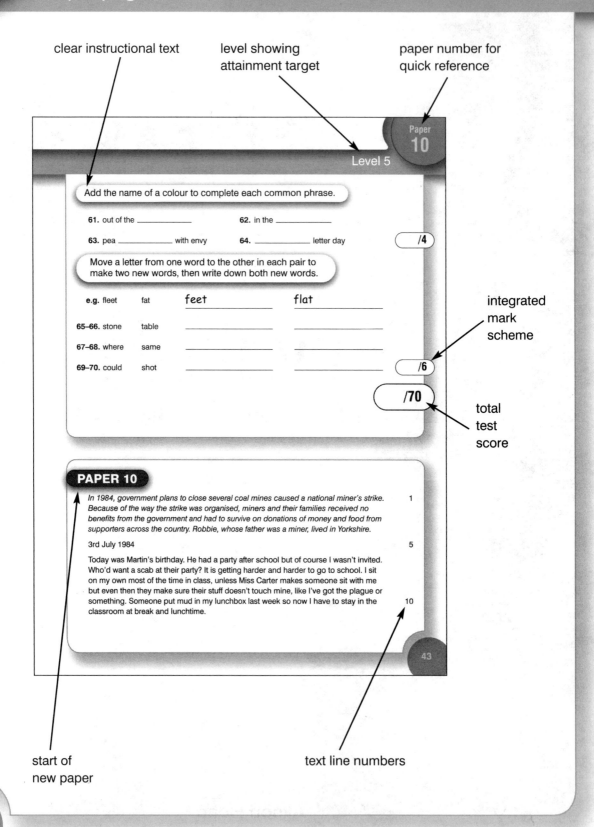

Paper 10

Level 5

Add the name of a colour to complete each common phrase.

61. out of the _____   **62.** in the _____

63. pea _____ with envy   **64.** _____ letter day   /4

Move a letter from one word to the other in each pair to make two new words, then write down both new words.

e.g. fleet   fat   feet   flat

65–66. stone   table   _____   _____

67–68. where   same   _____   _____

69–70. could   shot   _____   _____   /6

/70

integrated mark scheme

total test score

PAPER 10

In 1984, government plans to close several coal mines caused a national miner's strike. 1
Because of the way the strike was organised, miners and their families received no
benefits from the government and had to survive on donations of money and food from
supporters across the country. Robbie, whose father was a miner, lived in Yorkshire.

3rd July 1984   5

Today was Martin's birthday. He had a party after school but of course I wasn't invited.
Who'd want a scab at their party? It is getting harder and harder to go to school. I sit
on my own most of the time in class, unless Miss Carter makes someone sit with me
but even then they make sure their stuff doesn't touch mine, like I've got the plague or
something. Someone put mud in my lunchbox last week so now I have to stay in the   10
classroom at break and lunchtime.

43

start of new paper

text line numbers

Contents

PAPER 1

Mary Seacole, 1805–1881

Mary Seacole was a pioneering nurse who overcame prejudice to play a crucial role in the Crimean War. Her story is one of extraordinary determination and bravery.

Mary was born in Jamaica in 1805. Her mother was Jamaican and her father was a Scottish soldier. As a mixed race woman she would have been free, but would not have been able to vote, hold public office or become a professional.

Her mother was a nurse, treating people with local herbal remedies, and Mary would play at nursing her toys and pets. By the age of 12, she was working alongside her mother.

Mary travelled a great deal, which would have been very unusual for a woman in those days. She added European nursing techniques to her own medical knowledge and returned to Jamaica where she opened a hotel in which she took care of sick and injured soldiers and their families.

In 1853, the Crimean War began. Mary decided that she wanted to help the British soldiers who were fighting against the Russians and travelled to England to offer her services as a nurse. She hoped to work in one of the hospitals being run in Turkey by Florence Nightingale, but her applications for work were turned down again and again. Undeterred by this discrimination, Mary paid for her own passage to Turkey

Florence Nightingale's hospitals were three day's sailing away from the fighting, so Mary decided she would find a way to help closer to the battlefields. Using her own money, she opened *British Hotel*, very close to the fighting in Balaclava. There she took care of sick and injured soldiers and ran a shop selling things like boots, saddles and tins of soup to the troops. She also helped on the battlefields themselves, sometimes under canon fire, and because of this bravery she was awarded medals by Britain, Turkey and France.

In 1856, at the end of the war, Mary returned to Britain with no money and in poor health. She had become very famous in Britain for her work and had many supporters here, including the Prince of Wales. They raised money for her and she wrote a best-selling book about her life called *The Wonderful Adventures of Mrs Seacole in Many Lands*. She died in 1881 and is buried in London.

Circle your answers.

1. What type of text is this?

biography   autobiography   fiction

2. Where was Mary Seacole born?

Scotland   Turkey   Jamaica

3. When did the Crimean War begin?

1805   1853   1856

4–5. Suggest two reasons why people would have been prejudiced against Mary Seacole.

_____

_____

6. Why do you think her applications to nurse in Florence Nightingale's hospitals were turned down?

_____

7–8. Suggest one advantage and one disadvantage of situating Florence Nightingale's hospitals three days away from the fighting.

advantage   _____

disadvantage   _____

9–10. Find one piece of evidence that demonstrates that Mary Seacole was brave and one piece that demonstrates that she was determined.

brave: _____

determined: _____

11. By the end of the Crimean War, Mary Seacole had lost all of her money. Find one piece of evidence to suggest that at the beginning of the war she would have been quite a wealthy woman.

_____

12. Why do you think Mary Seacole's book was a bestseller?

_____ /12

Write these words in alphabetical order.

distance   distribute   disturb   distraction   distil   distinctive

13–18. _____   _____   _____

_____   _____   _____ /6

Underline the **main clause** in each **complex sentence**.

19. My sister broke her ankle when she went skiing.

20. Max finished his project before he started his homework.

21. Amy got up early to make sure she would not be late.

22. Robbie waited in his classroom until the teacher was ready to speak to him.

23. After she had made sure it was safe, Ella crossed the road.

24. Because she had forgotten her bus money, Sarah had to walk home.

/6

Add the missing vowel to each word.

25. med___l

26. bagg___ge

27. c___mpare

28. r___lation

29. diff___rent

30. d___pend

31. ed___ble

32. fact___ry

/8

Draw lines to match up the two halves of each **proverb**.

33. Many hands   by its cover.

34. Too many cooks   until they are hatched.

35. Every cloud   catches the worm.

36. Don't count your chickens   make light work.

37. The early bird   spoil the broth.

38. Don't judge a book   has a silver lining.

/6

Add the **suffix** to each word, making any necessary changes to spelling.

39. grace + full = _____

40. hope + ing = _____

41. safe + er = _____

42. achieve + able = _____

43. brave + ly = _____

44. big + er = _____

45. face + ing = _____

46. rely + able = _____   /8

Write down the masculine form of each word.

47. women _____   **48.** vixen _____

49. queen _____   **50.** cow _____

51. niece _____   **52.** princess _____

53. aunt _____   **54.** duchess _____   /8

Write down an **antonym** for each word.

55. innocent _____   **56.** find _____

57. freeze _____   **58.** understand _____

59. subtract _____   **60.** wide _____

61. ascent _____   **62.** stale _____   /8

Add the missing commas to these sentences.

63–64. We added sweet corn onion pepper and mushrooms to our pizza.

65–67. I went to the cinema with Jack Mark Andrew Martin and Joe.

68–70. The train stopped at Reading Bristol Bath Taunton and Yeovil.   /8

/70

PAPER 2

Tides

I watch children play in their holes in the sand   1
In this magical place, between sea and land.
A racing car, a submarine,
anything that they can dream.
And then I send in my foam-frilled potion   5
to take their hole back to the ocean.

Called by the moon to behave in this way
Washing the beach with its waves twice a day,
Removing all traces of splendid sandcastles
and stealing the crumbs from the folk, who with parcels   10
Of filled rolls and cakes and flasks of tea
Picnic on the beach and gaze out to sea.

The beach, remember, belongs to me,
and I'll take it, whenever I choose, to the sea.
I clean it and polish it, smooth and new.   15
then lend it, again, to folk like you.

Circle your answers.

1. Where is the hole described in line 1?

    under the sea   on the beach   on the moon

2. How many times does the tide come in each day?

    1   2   3

3. Who does the poem say the beach belongs to?

    the folk   the moon   the tides

Answer these questions.

4. What are the children doing on the beach?

_____

5. Why might they find it a *magical place* (line 2)?

_____

6. What does the poem says causes the tides?

_____

7. Find and copy an example of alliteration.

_____

8. Find and copy an example of personification.

_____

9. What important job does the poem say that the tide does?

_____

10. Find a word in the poem that means people.

_____   /10

Underline the correct **homophone** to complete each sentence.

11. The girls had (there their) hair cut.

12. "(Wear Where) are you going?" asked Dad.

13. I was (too to) full to finish my ice cream.

14. (Their There) is going to be a solar eclipse next week.

15. Sally couldn't decide (which witch) shoes to wear.

16. My friends are great because (their they're) lots of fun.

17. Our dog hides (its it's) toys behind the sofa.

18. I don't (no know) where my coat is.   /8

Sort the words into the chart.

19–30.   field   leap   funny   rapidly   they   us

sad   cheerfully   see   sea   from   beyond

noun	adjective	verb	adverb	pronoun	preposition

/12

Underline the **onomatopoeia** in these sentences.

31. We warmed ourselves by the roaring fire.

32. The pile of boxes fell over with a crash.

33. The tissue paper rustled as I unwrapped the present.

34. The speeding car came to a screeching halt.

35. Rain pattered on the umbrella.

36. The baby gurgled happily in its pram.

/6

Write down a **synonym** for each word.

37. lost _____

38. funny _____

39. throw _____

40. dirty _____

41. follow _____

42. elegant _____

43. answer _____

44. mean _____

/8

Use lines to join each word to its **definition**.

45. hail   a major road with several lanes of traffic

46. pet   a place where sick people go to get better

47. motorway   frozen rain

48. lane   a room for storing and preparing food

49. hospital   a minor road or small track

50. kitchen   an animal kept for fun

/6

Add the **prefix** *un* or *im* to each word.

51. _____realistic

52. _____modest

53. _____necessary

54. _____port

55. _____possible

56. _____natural

57. _____expected

58. _____mature

/8

Complete these **similes**.

59. as dry as   _____   **60.** as cunning as _____

61. as pretty as   _____   **62.** as white as   _____

63. as bold as   _____   **64.** as quick as   _____

65. as blind as   _____   **66.** as fresh as   _____   /8

Write these statements again, as questions. E.g. The boys are playing football. Are the boys playing football?

67. Carrie loves going to the cinema.   _____

68. Dad will be back in time for dinner.   _____

69. We should put a coat on.   _____

70. It is raining today.   _____   /4

/70

PAPER 3

My Dear Agatha,

You cannot imagine with what sadness I heard of the death of our dearest Uncle Arthur.   1
Naturally I was aware that he had been in failing health for some time and I had, of
course, fully intended to visit you both. However, you cannot know how busy my little
family keeps me.

Indeed, Uncle did himself write to me, imploring me to relieve you of your nursing duties   5
for a short while, to give you a chance to rest. I smiled to myself at his misunderstanding
of my situation here. As if I could leave my home here to run all by itself! A housekeeper
and nanny are all very well, but without my tireless attention, I swear we would all

descend into chaos in no time at all. I am certain dear Uncle knew that I have always been
just as devoted to his care and wellbeing as you.   10

Still, I suppose now you can have all the rest that you want.

Dear sister, I hate to think of you alone in that huge, gloomy house, filled all around by
Uncle's treasures. I am sure that it must make you feel his loss all the more to be always
surrounded by his books and paintings, however valuable they may be.

Knowing me to be a devoted niece I am certain he would have wanted me to share in the   15
burden of caring for some of his more valuable possessions. That is not to say, of course,
that he would not want you to benefit in some small way for your nursing of him for the past
four years. It is just that as the eldest sister I may naturally expect a significant inheritance.

I beg you to send me a speedy reply.

Yours always,   20

Bella

Underline your answers.

1. What relation was Arthur to Agatha and Bella?

  father   uncle   brother

2. How long had Agatha been nursing Arthur?

  4 years   5 years   10 years

3. Which sister still lives in Arthur's house?

  Agatha   Bella   neither of them

4. Looking at the language used in the letter, do you think it was written recently,
or a long time ago? Give a reason for your answer.

_____

5. Bella says that she was just as devoted to Arthur's care as Agatha was.
Do you think this is true? Give a reason for your answer.

_____

6–7. Which two people are employed to help Bella to run her home?

_____ _____

8. Do you think Bella could have found the time to visit Arthur and Agatha?

_____

9. Which of the two sisters is the oldest?

_____

10. Do you think Arthur was a wealthy man? Find evidence in the letter to support your answer.

_____

11. What does the word _inheritance_ (line 18) mean?

_____

12. Which sister do you think deserves to get more of Arthur's money and possessions? Give a reason for your answer.

_____

/12

Underline the **root word** in each of these words.

13. submarine
14. localise

15. realise
16. careful

17. redesign
18. employment

19. measurement
20. transplant

/8

Write the word **active** or **passive** after each sentence.

21. The shoes were chewed by the puppy. _____

22. The shed was damaged by the wind. _____

23. Our teacher handed out the books. _____

24. The vase was broken by my little brother. _____

25. Katie scored the winning goal. _____

26. Some children fed bread to the ducks. _____

/6

Write these sentences again, adding the capital letters and punctuation.

27–32. when she was nine eve moved to england from france

_____

33–36. alis birthday is in october

_____ /10

> Add a suitable **pronoun** to complete each sentence.

37. Alfie was kept in at break because _____ was talking in class.

38. Beth and I are going shopping later because _____ need new shoes.

39. When _____ got home, the boys were very hungry.

40. The lock was stiff because _____ needed oiling.

41. Mum's car broke down so Dad went to collect _____.

42. Claire always does her homework as soon as _____ gets home from school.

43. Mark was ill so his mum made _____ go to bed.

44. The sea was too rough for _____ to go swimming. /8

> Write the **plurals** of these words.

45. box _____ **46.** wolf _____

47. bush _____ **48.** bear _____

49. party _____ **50.** monkey _____

51. house _____ **52.** tomato _____ /8

> Write these sentences again, without the double negatives.

53. My book wasn't nowhere to be found.

_____

54. Jamie went to get some milk but there wasn't none left.

_____

55. The mechanic said there wasn't nothing wrong with the car.

_____

56. Caitlin said that she hadn't done nothing wrong.

_____ /4

> Write down two words which end with each **suffix**.

57–58. graph   _____   _____

59–60. port   _____   _____

61–62. ology   _____   _____

63–64. scope   _____   _____   /8

> Write these words again, with the correct spelling.

65. intrested   _____

66. easely   _____

67. originul   _____

68. diffrence   _____

69. freedum   _____

70. genarous   _____   /6

/70

PAPER 4

Five of us slept in that little room. At six, I was the youngest. The oldest was Billy, who was nearly 11 but very small for his age. Ernie kept us short of food to keep us skinny and over the years this seemed to have the effect of keeping us short, too. It's not nice to be hungry but, as Ernie was fond of saying, it isn't nice to be out of work either. The fact is, the longer we stayed small, the longer we'd be useful as sweeps.

Nobody would ever talk about what happened to sweeps who got too big. I decided I'd watch as Billy grew but that never happened. He fell down a flue and broke his neck on his 12th birthday. Around the same time, Ernie told us of a boy who'd stolen broth and bread from the kitchen of a house he was sweeping. Turns out the food he had taken was so rich it made him grow and soon after he got stuck in a chimney and choked to death. So stay small or grow, there didn't seem much for us to look forward to.

That first year was terribly hard. I missed my family dreadfully, and though the other boys did their best to comfort me, I would have cried myself to sleep each night, except I was too tired for that.

It's hard to describe what it is like when you go up a chimney for the first time. It is the darkest thing you can imagine and every breath you take catches dry in your throat. Since chimneys must be cleaned, it seems strange that they should be built so narrow. Although I was small, at six, that first chimney gripped my terrified body so tight that I was sure I'd be stuck fast. I cried out and begged Ernie to pull me out by my feet but instead he reached up the chimney with a lighted taper and singed my toes, as encouragement to keep going.

I was so afraid of going on that I hung there debating which was worse, coming down and being beaten and cast out to an uncertain fate, or climbing further up and getting stuck. Of course, I chose to climb. I knew that the streets of London were not kind to little boys. That chimney took the skin off my knees and elbows and I hadn't enough tears to wash the soot from my eyes.

1

5

10

15

20

25

Circle your answers.

1. Who was the oldest boy who slept in the room?

    Ernie   Billy   Bob

2. How old is the narrator?

    nearly 11   6   12

3. Why doesn't the narrator cry himself to sleep?

    he has soot in his eyes   the other boys comfort him   he is too tired

4–5. How does Ernie treat the boys? Find two pieces of evidence to support your answer.

_____

_____

6. Why does Ernie want to keep the boys small?

_____

7–8. Find two reasons why the narrator doesn't know what happened to boys who got too big.

_____

_____

9. According to Ernie, what caused the chimneysweep to get stuck up the chimney and choke?

_____

10. What does the narrator say is strange about the way chimneys are built?

_____

11. What is unusual about the use of the word *encouragement*? (line 23)

_____

12. Why does the narrator decide to keep climbing the chimney?

_____ /12

From each **noun**, make a **verb** ending in *ise.*

13. magnet _____

14. liquid _____

15. critic _____

16. television _____

17. advert _____

18. priority _____ /6

Add a suitable **main clause** to complete each sentence.

19. When she felt better, _____.

20. _____ before he had time to think.

21. Although she was tired, _____.

22. _____, as he opened the door.

23. As quickly as they could, _____.

24. While I was sleeping, _____.   /6

Circle the words that have entered the English language in the past 50 years.

25–32.			
emoticon	blog	submarine	widescreen
radio	chalet	broadband	website
circus	telephone	ringtone	aeroplane
wannabe	Euro	footballer	bonfire

/8

Write these sentences again, as **reported speech**.

33. "Are you two hungry?" asked Dad.

_____

34. Mum said, "I'll get some milk on the way home."

_____

35. "Layla, have you seen my watch?" asked Jessica.

_____

36. The teacher shouted, "It's too noisy in here!"

_____

37. "It's snowing!" exclaimed Jack.

_____

38. Gran suggested, "We could go to the cinema later."

_____   /6

Write down the words that each **contraction** stands for.

39. he's   _____   **40.** wouldn't   _____

41. she'll _____ **42.** shan't _____

43. they've _____ **44.** won't _____

45. it's _____ **46.** I'll _____ /8

Write down what **tense** each sentence is written in.

47. It will be great to see you on Saturday. _____

48. Mr Fryer was angry because I hadn't done my homework. _____

49. Our teacher was off school yesterday. _____

50. My house is being extended at the moment. _____

51. The school football team plays really well. _____

52. I will be 11 on my next birthday. _____ /6

Complete these **metaphors**.

53. The apples were red _____.

54. The storm was an angry _____.

55. The lake was a smooth _____.

56. The frost was a _____ coating on the ground.

57. _____ was a wild animal, roaring.

58. _____ were eyes in the front of the house. /6

Underline the silent letter in each word.

59. knife **60.** biscuit

61. gnome **62.** tongue

63. guess **64.** design

65. Autumn **66.** handkerchief /8

Write a sentence using each **preposition**.

67. against   _____

68. across   _____

69. inside   _____

70. for   _____   /4

/70

PAPER 5

The Biofuel debate

Today, most of the energy we use comes from fossil fuels like coal, oil and natural gases. These have been produced over millions of years from the remains of plants and animals that lived long ago. Because we are using them many times faster than they are produced, these fuels will eventually run out. Fuels like this are called non-renewable, because we can't make them again.

There is another problem with fossil fuels. To release the energy they contain they have to be burned and that is very bad for the environment.

In the future, we will have to use other sources of energy. One possibility is using biofuels. These are fuels made from plants like sugar cane. Because we can keep growing new plants this type of fuel is described as renewable. We would never run out of biofuel, although just like fossil fuels, they have to be burned to release their energy.

However, many people are worried about biofuels because as we use so much fuel, we would need to grow plants over enormous areas. Already land that was used to grow food, and large areas of forests, is being cleared to grow biofuels. Some people think that this makes biofuels just as bad for the environment at fossil fuels. They argue that instead of replacing fossil fuel with biofuel, we should try to find ways to use less fuel.

In addition, although it is the richest countries in the world that use the most fuel, it is the developing countries that are growing most of the biofuel crops. Many people worry that the environment in these countries is being damaged and that people there could go hungry if not enough food is grown.

On the other hand, growing biocrops earns some of these countries a lot of money that they could use to make life better for the people who live there.

Research into biofuels and other renewable energy sources, like solar, wave or wind power, continues and the debate over which is best looks set to continue. One thing is certain however, we cannot continue to rely on fossil fuels for our energy because one day they will simply not be there.

Circle your answers.

1. Today, where does most of our energy come from?

wind power   fossil fuels   sugar cane

2. Circle a renewable energy source.

coal   gas   solar power

3. Which of these is sometimes cleared to grow biofuel?

forests   towns   coal mines

4. Why do you think fuels like coal, oil and gas are called *fossil fuels*?

_____

5–6. List two problems with fossil fuels.

_____

_____

7. As well as biofuels, find another renewable energy source the text mentions.

_____

8. Find one thing that fossil fuels and biofuels have in common.

_____

9. How would it help the environment if we all used less energy, whether it comes from fossil fuels or biofuels?

_____

10–11. Describe one possible advantage and one possible disadvantage to a developing country which grows crops to make biofuel.

_____

_____

12. Why do you think the richest countries do not choose to grow biofuels?

_____   /12

Add another word to the beginning or end of each of these, to make a **compound word.**

13. bag   _____   14. hedge   _____

15. wheel   _____   16. cup   _____

17. chair   _____   18. man   _____

19. tree   _____   20. fire   _____   /8

Underline the **conditional clause** in each sentence.

21. If it snows, we will go sledging.

22. Should our train be delayed, we will miss the concert.

23. I will move up to the next group if I pass the test.

24. I'll bring your book back tomorrow if I can find it.

25. I would have left earlier had I known the car would break down.

26. If I were you, I would start that piece of work again.   /6

Add the **suffix** ible or able to each word, making any necessary changes to spelling.

27. fashion   _____   28. agree   _____

29. reverse   _____   30. sense   _____

31. access   _____   32. value   _____

30. reason _____   **34.** response _____

/8

Underline the **subject** of each sentence.

35. Rory kicked the ball straight into the goal.

36. The children cried because they were tired.

37. Mum drove Sally to her drama class.

38. After tea, the boys played on the computer.

39. The snow covered everything with a soft, white blanket.

40. The girl was very late for school.

/6

Underline the **root word**, then write
another word that shares the same root.

41–42. clearly _____

43–44. manageable _____

45–46. used _____

47–48. friendship _____

49–50. lovely _____

/10

Add the speech marks to these sentences.

51–52. Did a letter arrive for me? asked Dad.

53–54. Ouch said Paige, pricking her finger on a thorn.

55–56. Molly queried, Are we nearly there?

/6

Write down two **adjectives** you could use to describe each thing.

57–58. a fairground ride _____   _____

59–60. an ice cream sundae _____   _____

61–62. a kitten's fur   _____   _____

63–64. a storm   _____   _____   **/8**

Add a suitable **adverb** to complete each sentence.

65. The children clapped _____ when the clowns came into the ring.

66. The lion bounded _____ towards the edge of its enclosure.

67. Bees buzzed _____ from flower to flower.

68. When the fire alarm sounds, we must leave the classroom _____.

69. The boy held the door open _____ for the man behind.

70. The stars twinkled _____ in the sky.   **/6**

/70

PAPER 6

Royal Theatre raises the roof

There's new hope for an old theatre after supporters raised enough money to repair its leaking   1
roof. Biddecomb's Royal Theatre was built in the 1860s but a lack of investment over the past
30 years has left the building crumbling. Now a group of local supporters have raised the
£500,000 needed to repair the roof and a bright future awaits.

     Publicity manager Dawn McGrath explains, "Local people have been fantastic and now   5
that we can keep the rain out, there is real hope for this beautiful old theatre. We have some
great shows coming up in the next few months including *The Tempest*, *An Inspector Calls* and
the pantomime *Peter Pan*."

     The theatre also plays host to TV's *Ghost Watch* this Friday, when the crew will be
broadcasting live from the theatre. They will be hoping to hear from Tilly Marne, who was a   10
ballerina at the theatre in the 1930s and is said to haunt the stage area. Tilly was badly injured
when some scenery fell on her during rehearsals for *Sleeping Beauty* and although she recovered,

she never danced again. A ballet company performing here in 1962 reportedly found their ballet shoes worn out one morning and since then people have claimed that Tilly returns to dance at night.

So are the TV crew in for a shock? "Personally, I don't think so," says Dawn. "Tilly went on to marry her childhood sweetheart. They emigrated to Canada and lived long happy lives. In 1962 she was alive and well and running a ballet school in Vancouver. If the TV show helps to publicise the theatre though, that can only be a good thing!"

An exhibition of old costumes worn in performances at the theatre, including a tutu worn by Tilly Marne, is being held at the Town Hall until the end of March. When it closes, the costumes will be auctioned to raise funds to repair the decorative plasterwork.

15

20

Circle your answers.

1. Which pantomime will play at the theatre?

Sleeping Beauty   *Peter Pan*   *The Tempest*

2. What was Tilly Marne's job?

ballerina   publicity manager   theatre supporter

3. When was the theatre built?

1860s   1930s   1962

Answer these questions.

4. Why might a 'lack of investment' in an old building be a particular problem?

_____

5. What happened to Tilly Marne in the theatre?

_____

6. Nobody really knows why, in 1962, a ballet company found their shoes worn out in the morning. Write a sentence suggesting what you think could have happened.

_____

7. In your own words, explain why Dawn McGrath does not think that Tilly haunts the theatre.

_____

8. What does the word *emigrated* mean in line 16?

_____

9. Why do you think Dawn McGrath says that publicity can only be a good thing?

_____

10. What will happen to the costumes in the exhibition when it has finished?

_____

11. Why do you think the newspaper article makes a special point of telling readers that Tilly Marne's tutu is appearing in the costume exhibition?

_____ /11

Put these words in reverse alphabetical order.

mistook mistake mistress mister misty mistletoe

12–17. _____ _____ _____

_____ _____ _____ /6

Add *ie* or *ei* to compete each word.

18. rel_____f   **19.** rec_____ve   **20.** h_____ght

21. bel_____ve   **22.** s_____ze   **23.** sh_____ld

24. rec_____pt /7

Write a **definition** for each of these words.

25. fact

_____

26. fiction

_____

27. opinion

_____ /3

Write down the **plurals** of these **nouns**.

28. calf _____   **29.** bone _____

30. pitch _____   **31.** sheep _____

32. ox _____   **33.** baby _____

34. mouse _____   **35.** gate _____   /8

Complete these well-known **similes**.

36. as blind as a _____

37. swim like a _____

38. as pleased as _____

39. cunning like a _____

40. as gentle as a _____   /5

Write these words again with the correct spelling.

41. goverment _____   **42.** rasberry _____

43. hanbag _____   **44.** miniture _____

45. vegtable _____   **46.** histry _____

47. seprate _____   **48.** Wenseday _____   /8

Add a suitable **conjunction** to complete each sentence.

49. Mum will be angry _____ I am late home.

50. Our dog stayed with my auntie _____ we got back from holiday.

51. We bought Alex a present _____ it was his birthday.

52. I wanted to make a sandwich _____ we had run out of bread.

53. I can't go out _____ I have finished my homework.

54. I was eight years old _____ we moved to this town.

/6

Add a **prefix** to each word to make a new word.

55. _____port

56. _____charge

57. _____vision

58. _____scope

59. _____cycle

60. _____arrange

61. _____graph

62. _____historic

/8

Use *was* or *were* to complete each sentence.

63. Amy _____ busy writing a story.

64. The children _____ playing hockey.

65. A flock of birds _____ roosting in the trees.

66. Eve's pictures _____ all over her bedroom walls.

67. Because the bus was late, Ali and Sam _____ late for school.

/5

Write a second clause to complete these sentences.

68. It began to snow while _____.

69. I lost my bag but _____.

70. We brushed our teeth before _____.

/3

/70

PAPER 7

As the coach drew up in the car park, it started to drizzle. The group was more than an hour late because of a jam on the motorway and the class was tired and fed up. Their guide met them and ushered them to the entrance of the caves for what she called 'the briefing'. This turned out to be a list of rules which was delivered to the group as they shivered in the rain, which was falling heavily by then. "Stay together, watch out for slippery surfaces and don't, under any circumstances, leave the lit route."

It all sounded so obvious and boring. Like Tom's mum said, if it was dangerous they would never let children go down there.

Inside the cave, things were a bit better. They were out of the pelting rain at least. Every now and then a spotlight would pick out a stalactite or other geological feature and the guide would pause to explain how it had formed. Lingering at the back of the group, and already restless from the dreadful journey, the three boys soon lost interest. They shone their torches into side passages and caverns and up into their faces to make them look scary.

Busily making shadow figures on the walls of the cave, the boys didn't notice the rest of the class filing off into the next chamber. As the guide's voice faded away, they missed her explaining how the unlit outlying tunnel system frequently flooded in heavy rain. They didn't hear how, out of more than 40 tunnels in the complex, only the very narrowest led back to the surface.

Five minutes later, surrounded by silence, the three boys realised they had been left behind. They raced into the next chamber, skidding on the slippery surface. Inside, they were faced with three tunnels. One, although well-lit, was so narrow that you would have to turn sideways in order to pass along it.

"They won't have gone in there," said Tom. "It must be one of the others."

"Let's try this one," suggested Luke. "There are a few lights down here. We'll go a little way in, and then if we can't hear them, we'll come back and try the other one."

It seemed like a good plan, but not far inside, the tunnel forked again. Only one passage was lit at all and after a few metres the lights fizzled out, and the boys decided to turn back. But then they reached another fork.

"It all looks different from this direction," said James. "Surely we should be heading back towards the surface, but all of these tunnels lead further down. We must have missed the right one, or we'd be able to hear the others."

The boys were starting to feel the chill now, in their damp clothes. They had eaten their packed lunches almost as soon as the coach left school and now they felt hungry. To make matters worse the tunnels, which were just damp when they had set off, were now submerged under a thin layer of water which was getting deeper all the time.

With a jolt of relief, Tom had an idea. He got out his mobile phone. "We'll just ring for help," he said, grinning. But of course, so far underground, there was no signal.

"We'll have to split up to look for a way out," said James, desperately.

Circle your answers.

1. What sort of group made the trip in the story?

    a family   a youth group   a school class

2. Where did the guide deliver 'the briefing?'

    at the cave entrance   in the coach   inside the caves

3. How many boys get lost in the cave system?

    the whole class   3   1

Answer these questions.

4. Find and copy a word that describes a type of rain.

_____

5. What did Tom's mother say that might have made him take the guide's warnings less seriously?

_____

6. How does the weather above the ground affect the risks the boys face in the caves?

_____

7. One of the passages the boys come across is well-lit. Why does Tom assume that the group won't have gone along it?

_____

8. How can the boys still see where they are going in the passages without electric lights?

_____

9–10. Apart from fear, find two ways in which the boys feel uncomfortable after they get lost.

_____

_____

11. Apart from the clothes they were wearing, the boys only had torches and a mobile phone. Write a sentence to explain which would have been more useful to them and why.

_____

12. Do you think it would be a good idea for the boys to split up to find a way out?
Write a sentence to explain why.

_____ /12

Write these sentences again with **passive verbs**.

13. The cat scratched the little girl.

_____

14. An owl's hoot shattered the silence.

_____

15. Tara wrote the best story.

_____

16. Mum built a rockery in the garden.

_____

17. Road works held up the traffic.

_____

18. The rain stopped the cricket match.

_____ /6

Write the **plurals** of these words.

19. person   _____   **20.** child   _____

21. goose   _____   **22.** man   _____

23. woodlouse _____   **24.** tooth   _____   /6

Write this piece of text again adding **punctuation**,
including **speech marks**. Remember to start a new
line each time a different person speaks.

25–40. Are we nearly there whined Oscar Not too much further replied Dad Can we go straight
to the beach when we get there begged Oscar If you like laughed Dad

_____

_____

_____

_____

_____ /16

Sort the words into the chart.

41–48.   heroine brother wife mother son king boar hen

masculine	feminine

/8

Write an **antonym** for each the bold words.

49. Mum was **happy** that Aunt Sarah was coming to stay. _____

50. **Fortunately**, a new road is being built to carry the extra traffic. _____

51. Dad is **buying** a car. _____

52. I am the **tallest** in my class. _____

53. The train to Birmingham is due to **arrive** at 3.15. _____

54. The maths homework was quite **difficult**. _____

/6

Add the missing words to complete each **abbreviation**.

55. PTO   please turn _____

56. GB   Great _____

57. UK   United _____

58. SOS   save our _____

59. USA   United _____ of America

60. HRH   His/Her Royal _____

/6

Unscramble these **anagrams** to reveal four parts of the body. Each word contains a silent letter.

61. eken   _____

62. btuhm   _____

63. kkleunc   _____

64. ldrehsou   _____

/4

Add a **preposition** to complete each well known phrase.

65. _____ the moon

66. _____ cloud nine

67. _____ the weather

68. _____ thick and thin

69. _____ safe hands

70. let the cat _____ of the bag

/6

/70

PAPER 8

Fan-tastic!

Westborough United honoured its oldest fan on Saturday with a charity match against   1
rivals Southborough FC.

Ernest Best, 98, was guest of honour at the match and watched the action from the
dugout. He saw his first football match at the age of just six years old and has been
a regular supporter ever since.   5

He explains: "As a young man I prided myself on never missing a home game. During
the war that all changed of course but when it was all over and I was back from France,
I couldn't wait to get to the ground to see a match. That was when I really knew I was
home. I remember that match like it was yesterday: a two nil victory against Bicester.
Pure magic!"   10

The club has certainly seem some changes during the years that Ernest has been
a supporter. One of the biggest was the move to the current ground, with its new
stadium, in 1994. That paved the way to the club becoming professional in 1998.
Whatever changes, insists Chairman Bob Finney, the club's supporters will always
play a key part in the success of the club.   15

"Without our supporters there would be no point getting out of bed in the morning.
Getting the boys out on the pitch in front of a big crowd is the best feeling in the
world. Knowing that we have a supporter who stuck with us through all our ups
and downs, for all those years, is really special."

Ernest is keeping his love of Westborough United in the family, too. His son, grandson   20
and great granddaughter all hold season tickets for the club.

Saturday's game raised £2,500 for Westborough hospital's renal unit. It was a closely
contested match with Westborough taking an early goal after just four minutes.
Southborough equalised just before half time before stealing a second goal just into
the second half, leaving Westborough with a lot to do. They rose to the challenge,   25
equalising just before the full time whistle and scoring a third goal two minutes into
extra time.

Ernest's verdict on the 3-2 final score? "Fantastic. Real 'edge of the seat' stuff!"

Circle your answers.

1. What does the abbreviation FC mean in the name Southborough FC?

   football coach   football club   football court

2. When did the football club move to its new ground?

   1998   1994   1949

3. What was the score in Saturday's football match?

3-2   2-0   3-3

Answer these questions.

4. Explain why the writer might have chosen the headline *Fan-tastic*.

_____

5. Why might the war have meant that Ernest couldn't go to all of the home matches?

_____

6. Why do you think he remembers the match against Bicester so vividly?

_____

7–8. List two major changes that have happened to the club since Ernest has been supporting it.

_____

_____

9. According to Chairman Bob Finney, what is the best feeling in the world?

_____

10. What is meant by the term *closely contested*. (line 22)

_____

11. Judging from the match report, which team played better in the second half?

_____

12. What does Ernest mean when he describes the match as *edge of the seat stuff* (line 28)?

_____

/12

Add the **suffix** *ery*, *ary* or *ory* to complete each word.

13. libr_____   **14.** bound_____   **15.** fact_____

16. batt_____   **17.** necess_____   **18.** categ_____

19. discov_____   **20.** nurs_____

/8

Write these **present tense** sentences again in the **past tense**.

21. I make my bed each morning.

_____

22. We always buy our sweets on Dean Street.

_____

23. Our class picture is in the local newspaper.

_____

24. Do you go to drama club?

_____

25. My little brother makes a mess in my bedroom.

_____

26. We always go to Bournemouth for our holidays.

_____   /6

Add the **apostrophes** in the correct places.

27. The suns rays are very bright.

28. The childrens paintings were very colourful.

29. A mans car would not start.

30. Three buildings shadows blotted out the sunshine.

31. The peoples cars filled the car park.

32. Some girls faces were decorated with face paints.

33. The boys mothers arranged an end of term party.

34. The sandwiches crusts were dry and stale.   /8

Write down two examples of each type of **noun**.

35–36. common nouns _____   _____

37–38. proper nouns   _____   _____

39–40. abstract nouns   _____   _____

41–42. collective nouns   _____   _____   /8

Write these sentences again, without the double negatives.

43. There wasn't nobody around when we got into town.

_____

44. I didn't see nothing in the playground.

_____

45. They couldn't see nothing in the darkness.

_____

46. There wasn't nowhere to escape from the cold.

_____

47. By lunchtime there wasn't no milk left.

_____

48. There weren't no parking spaces left in the car park.

_____   /6

Circle the **adjective** that can be made from each noun.

49.	**France**	French	Frances
50.	**genius**	generous	ingenious
51.	**mischief**	mischievous	mischiefer
52.	**aggression**	aggressive	agress
53.	**reason**	reasonable	raisin
54.	**ability**	ableous	able
55.	**circle**	circler	circular
56.	**hero**	heroic	heroes

   /8

Add a **semi-colon** to separate the clauses in each sentence.

57. The football match was cancelled the rain had flooded the pitch, leaving it dangerous.

58. I need to buy lots of things for school a new pencil case, notebooks, a calculator and an ink pen.

59. Jenny has one big ambition to visit China.

60. Robbie had two daily chores to do before school make his bed and feed his guinea pigs.

61. I have invited five friends to my party Sarah, Heather, Cherie and Laura.

62. Dad talks about the same thing all the time football.

/6

Write a **definition** for these words.

63. autobiography _____

64. biography _____

/2

Underline the embedded clause in each sentence.

65. The classes in year 6, who did not have a school trip last year, are visiting a theme park next week.

66. Car engines need to use fuel, which is often petrol, to make them run.

67. Finally, just as the boys were giving up hope, the lights of the lifeboat appeared through the fog.

68. Fruit and vegetables, which can include frozen or canned varieties, are good for your health.

69. In the end, although she had worked as quickly as she could, Bella ran out of time.

70. My cousins, who live in Canada, are spending the summer with us.

/6

/70

Answer booklet English 10–11

Paper 1
1. biography
2. Jamaica
3. 1853
4–5. She was a woman; she was of mixed race
6. because of racial prejudice.
7–8. Advantage: It would have been safe from the fighting Disadvantage: it was a long way for injured men to travel
9–10. Brave: she helped the soldiers even under fire Determined: she didn't give up when nobody would accept her help
11. She was able to pay for her passage to the Crimea and to set up her hotel with her own money.
12. Because she had led a very unusual life for a woman at that time and had helped a lot of people.
13–18. distance, distil, distinctive, distraction, distribute, disturb
19. My sister broke her ankle when she went skiing.
20. Max finished his project before he started his homework.
21. Amy got up early to make sure she would not be late.
22. Robbie waited in his classroom until the teacher was ready to speak to him.
23. After she had made sure it was safe, Ella crossed the road.
24. Because she had forgotten her bus money, Sarah had to walk home.
25. medal
26. baggage
27. compare
28. relation
29. different
30. depend
31. edible
32. factory
33. Many hands make light work.
34. Too many cooks spoil the broth.
35. Every cloud has a silver lining.
36. Don't count your chickens before they are hatched.
37. The early bird catches the worm.
38. Don't judge a book by its cover.
39. graceful
40. hoping
41. safer
42. achievable
43. bravely
44. bigger
45. facing
46. reliable
47. men
48. king
49. nephew
50. uncle
51. fox
52. bull
53. prince
54. duke
55. guilty
56. lose
57. thaw
58. misunderstand
59. add
60. narrow
61. descent
62. fresh
63–64. We added sweetcorn, onion, pepper and mushrooms to our pizza.
65–67. I went to the cinema with Jack, Mark, Andrew, Martin and Joe.
68–70. The train stopped at Reading, Bristol, Bath, Taunton and Yeovil.

Paper 2
1. on the beach
2. 2
3. the tides
4. The children are playing in the sand.
5. Because they can imagine all sorts of things there.
6. the moon
7. foam-frilled/splendid sandcastles
8. stealing the crumbs/it reminds us
9. it cleans the beach
10. folk
11. their
12. Where
13. too
14. There
15. which

16. they're
17. its
18. know
19–30. noun: field, sea
       adjective: funny, sad
       verb: leap, see
       adverb: rapidly, cheerfully
       pronoun: us, they
       preposition: from, beyond
31. roaring
32. crash
33. rustled
34. screeching
35. pattered
36. gurgled
37–44. answers may include:
37. misplaced
38. amusing
39. hurl
40. messy
41. chase
42. graceful
43. reply
44. horrid
45. frozen rain
46. an animal kept for fun
47. a major road with several lanes of traffic
48. a minor road or small track
49. a place where sick people go to get better
50. a room for storing and preparing food.
51. unrealistic
52. immodest
53. unnecessary
54. import
55. impossible
56. unnatural
57. unexpected
58. immature
59. as dry as a bone
60. as cunning as a fox
61. as pretty as a picture
62. as white as a sheet/snow
63. as bold as brass
64. as quick as a flash/lightning
65. as blind as a bat
66. as fresh as a daisy
67. Does Carrie love going to the cinema?
68. Will Dad be back in time for dinner?
69. Should we put a coat on?
70. Is it raining today?

Paper 3
1. uncle
2. 4 years
3. Agatha
4. a long time ago, because it includes old-fashioned language, e.g. dearest uncle, Indeed.
5. Answers may include: No, because she never found the time to visit him.
6–7. a nanny, a housekeeper
8. Answers may include: Yes, because she had plenty of help to run her home.
9. Bella
10. Yes, because Bella mentions his 'treasures' and 'valuable possessions and inheritance.
11. Something given to you when someone dies.
12. Answers may include: Agatha, because she took care of Uncle Arthur.
13. submarine
14. localise
15. realise
16. careful
17. redesign
18. employment
19. measurement
20. transplant
21. passive
22. passive
23. active
24. passive
25. active
26. ids active, ducks passive
27–32. When she was nine, Eve moved to England from France.
33–36. Ali's birthday is in October.
37. he
38. we
39. they
40. it
41. her or it
42. she
43. him
44. us
45. boxes

46. wolves
47. bushes
48. bears
49. parties
50. monkeys
51. houses
52. tomatoes
53. My book was nowhere to be found./ My book wasn't anywhere to be found.
54. Jamie went to get some milk but there was none left./ Jamie went to get some milk but there wasn't any left.
55. The mechanic said there was nothing wrong with the car. / The mechanic said there wasn't anything wrong with the car.
56. Caitlin said that she hadn't done anything wrong./ Caitlin said that she had done nothing wrong.
57–63. Answers might include:
57–58. photograph, telegraph
59–60. export, import
61–62. biology, geology
63–64. telescope, microscope
65. interested
66. easily
67. original
68. difference
69. freedom
70. generous

Paper 4
1. Billy
2. 6
3. he is too tired
4–5. Answer might include: He treats them badly. He doesn't give them enough to eat and burns the narrator's foot to make him climb the chimney.
6. So that they will stay small enough to fit up a chimney.
7–8. Nobody ever talks about it and the narrator didn't see what would happen when Billy grew too big because he died first.
9. He stole food which made him grow too big.
10. That although they need to be cleaned, they are built to narrow.
11. Encouragement is usually a positive thing but here it is cruel.
12. He decided it would be better to risk getting stuck up the chimney than to be left on the streets of London on his own.
13. magnetise
14. liquidise
15. criticise
16. televise
17. advertise
18. prioritise
19–24. Possible answers include:
19. When she felt better, Jenny got out of bed.
20. He opened his mouth before he had time to think.
21. Although she was tired, Claire kept watching TV.
22. Everyone shouted "Happy birthday!" as he opened the door.
23. As quickly as they could, the boys clambered over the wall.
24. While I was sleeping, the telephone rang.
25–32. emoticon, blog, widescreen, broadband, website, ringtone, wannabe, Euro
33. Dad asked us if we were hungry.
34. Mum said she would get some milk on the way home.
35. Jessica asked Layla if she had seen her watch.
36. The teacher shouted that it was too noisy.
37. Jack exclaimed that it was snowing.
38. Gran suggested that we went to the cinema later.
39. he is
40. would not
41. she will
42. shall not
43. they have
44. would not
45. it is
46. I will
47. future
48. past
49. past
50. present
51. present
52. future
53–58. Possible answers include:
53. The apples were red jewels.
54. The storm was an angry bear.

55. The lake was a smooth mirror.
56. The frost was a diamond coating on the ground.
57. The wind was a wild animal, roaring.
58. The windows were eyes in the front of the house.
59. knife
60. biscuit
61. gnome
62. tongue
63. guess
64. design
65. Autumn
66. handkerchief
67–70. sentences will vary

Paper 5
1. fossil fuels
2. solar power
3. forests
4. Because they are formed over millions of years from dead plants and animals.
5–6. They are non-renewable and burning them damages the environment.
7. any of solar, wind or wave power
8. They both have to be burnt.
9. We would need to burn less fuel to produce the energy we need.
10–11. Disadvantage: They may not have enough land to grow the biofuel crop and food to eat.
   Advantage: Selling biofuel crops would earn a lot of money for the country.
12. Because they know that they can afford to buy biofuel from other countries without needing to damage the environment in their own country.
13–20. Possible answers include:
13. handbag
14. hedgerow
15. wheelchair
16. cupcake
17. chairman
18. fireman
19. treetop
20. firework
21. If it snows, we will go sledging.
22. Should our train be delayed, we will miss the concert.
23. I will move up to the next group if I pass the test.
24. I'll bring your book back tomorrow if I can find it.
25. I would have left earlier had I known the car would break down.
26. If I were you, I would start that piece of work again.
27. fashionable
28. agreeable
29. reversible
30. sensible
31. accessible
32. valuable
33. reasonable
34. responsible
35. Rory kicked the ball straight into the goal.
36. The children cried because they were tired.
37. Mum drove Sally to her drama class.
38. After tea, the boys played on the computer.
39. The snow covered everything with a soft, white blanket.
40. The girl was very late for school.
41–50. Possible words include:
41–42. clearly, unclear
43–44. manageable, manager
45–46. used, useful
47–48. friendship, friendly
49–50. lovely, loved
51–52. "Did a letter arrive for me?" asked Dad.
53–54. "Ouch!" said Paige, pricking her finger with a thorn.
55–56. Molly queried, "Are we nearly there?"
57–64. Possible answers include:
57–58. bustling, colourful
59–60. delicious, sweet
61–62. soft, downy
63–64. deafening, powerful
65–70. Possible answers include:
65. excitedly
66. swiftly
67. busily
68. calmly
69. politely
70. brightly

Paper 6
1. Peter Pan
2. ballerina

3. 1860s
4. Old buildings tend to need a lot of expensive repairs.
5. She was injured when some scenery fell on her.
6. Sentences will vary.
7. Because in 1962, when people thought her ghost had worn out the ballet shoes, she was alive and well.
8. Go to live in another country.
9. If lots of people know about the theatre they will sell more tickets and raise more money.
10. They will be auctioned to raise money to repair the theatre's decorative plasterwork.
11. Because people will be interested in buying Tilly's tutu as a result of the ghost story that surrounds her.
12–17. misty, mistress, mistook, mistletoe, mister, mistake
18. relief
19. receive
20. height
21. believe
22. seize
23. shield
24. receipt
25. Something that can be shown to be true.
26. A made up story.
27. Someone's point of view on a topic.
28. calves
29. bones
30. pitches
31. sheep
32. oxen
33. babies
34. mice
35. gates
36. bat
37. fish
38. punch
39. fox
40. lamb
41. government
42. raspberry
43. handbag
44. miniature
45. vegetable
46. history
47. separate
48. Wednesday
49–54. Possible answers include:
49. if
50. until
51. because
52. but
53. before
54. when
55–62. Possible answers include:
55. export
56. recharge
57. revision
58. telescope
59. bicycle
60. rearrange
61. photograph
62. prehistoric
63. was
64. were
65. were
66. were
67. were
68–70. Possible answers include:
68. It began to snow while we were walking home.
69. I lost my bag but Dan found it again.
70. We brushed out teeth before we went to bed.

Paper 7
1. a school class
2. at entrance
3. 3
4. drizzle
5. That if the caves were dangerous, they wouldn't let groups of children inside.
6. When it rains heavily, the tunnels flood.
7. Because it is very narrow.
8. Because they have torches.
9–10. cold, hungry
11. Answers may vary but could include: The torch would be more useful because it would enable them to see in the dark, whereas the mobile phone would not be able to get a signal under the ground.
12. Answers may vary but could include: It would be a bad idea for the boys to split up to look for a way out because it was be harder to find three boys lost separately than three together.
13. The little girl was scratched by the cat.

14. The silence was shattered by an owl's hoot.
15. The best story was written by Tara.
16. A rockery was built in the garden by Mum.
17. The traffic was held up by road works.
18. The cricket match was stopped by the rain.
19. people
20. children
21. geese
22. men
23. woodlice
24. teeth
25–40. "Are we nearly there?" whined Oscar.
   "Not too much further," replied Dad.
   "Can we go straight to the beach when we get there?" begged Oscar.
   "If you like," laughed Dad.
41–48. Masculine: brother, son, king, boar
   Feminine: heroine, wife, mother, hen
49. Mum was unhappy that Aunt Sarah was coming to stay.
50. Unfortunately, a new road is being built to carry the extra traffic.
51. Dad is selling a car.
52. I am the shortest in my class.
53. The train to Birmingham is due to leave/depart at 3.15.
54. The maths homework was quite easy.
55. please turn over
56. Great Britain
57. United Kingdom
58. save our souls
59. United States of America
60. His/Her Royal Highness
61. knee
62. thumb
63. knuckle
64. shoulder
65. over
66. on
67. under
68. through
69. in
70. out

Paper 8
1. football club
2. 1994
3. 3-2
4. The headline is word play on the word fan, and the word fantastic that Ernest uses to describe the football match.
5. Because he would probably have been away fighting.
6. Because he was very glad to be home and hadn't seen a football match for a long time.
7–8. They move to a new ground and became a professional club.
9. Starting a football match in front of a big crowd.
10. It means that both teams were evenly-matched and both fought hard to win the game.
11. Westborough
12. It means he was so tense and excited that he couldn't sit on his seat properly but was ready to stand up and cheer all the time.
13. library
14. boundary
15. factory
16. battery
17. necessary
18. category
19. discovery
20. nursery
21. I made my bed each morning.
22. We always bought our sweets from the shop on Dean Street.
23. Our class picture was in the local newspaper.
24. Did you go to drama club?
25. My little brother made a mess in my bedroom.
26. We always went to Bournemouth for our holidays.
27. The sun's rays are very bright.
28. The children's paintings were very colourful.
29. A man's car would not start.
30. Three buildings' shadows blotted out the sunshine.
31. The people's cars filled the car park.
32. Some girls' faces were decorated with face paints.
33. The boys' mothers arranged an end of term party.
34. The sandwiches' crusts were dry and stale.
35–42. Possible answers include:
35–36. pen   cow
37–38. Belfast   November
39–40. happiness   knowledge
41–42. herd   pack

2

43. There was nobody around when we got into town./ There wasn't anybody around when we got into town.
44. I didn't see anything in the playground./ I saw nothing in the playground.
45. They couldn't see anything in the darkness. / They could see nothing in the darkness.
46. There wasn't anywhere to escape from the cold. / There was nowhere to escape from the cold.
47. By lunchtime there was no milk left. / By lunchtime there wasn't any milk left.
48. There weren't any parking spaces left in the car park. There were no parking spaces left in the car park.
49. French
50. ingenious
51. mischievous
52. aggressive
53. reasonable
54. able
55. circular
56. heroic
57. The football match was cancelled; the rain had flooded the pitch, leaving it dangerous.
58. I need to buy lots of things for school; a new pencil case, notebooks, a calculator and an ink pen.
59. Jenny has one big ambition; to visit China.
60. Robbie had two daily chores to do before school; make his bed and feed his guinea pigs.
61. I have invited five friends to my party, Sarah, Heather, Cherie and Laura.
62. Dad talks about the same thing all the time; football.
63. the story of someone's life, written by themselves
64. the story of someone's life, written by someone else
65. The classes in year 6, who did not have a school trip last year, are visiting a theme park next week.
66. Car engines need to use fuel, which is often petrol, to make them run.
67. Finally, just as the boys were giving up hope, the lights of the lifeboat appeared through the fog.
68. Fruit and vegetables, which can include frozen or canned varieties, are good for your health.
69. In the end, although she had worked as quickly as she could, Bella ran out of time.
70. My cousins, who live in Canada, are spending the summer with us.

Paper 9
1. Miss Smith
2. two terms
3. green 2.8
4. ruining their lessons, a bit at a time
5. The children feel that ruining a cover teacher's lessons is as enjoyable as eating something really delicious.
6–7. colouring and handwriting
8–9. military precision, laid out in regiments
10. Miss Smith looks very smart and is so organised that the children find it hard to be naughty. Miss Mess is less formally dressed, so the children may think that she will be disorganised and not be able to keep control.
11. Going straight across, from left to right, like the horizon.
12. No, because they have always managed to spoil the lessons of other cover teachers but Miss Mess seems able to control the class in some way.
13. did
14. done
15–16. did, done
17–18. done, did
19. grasshopper
20. peppermint
21. goldfish
22. sunshine
23. eggshell
24. wheelbarrow
25. waterfall
26. beehive
27–41. "Settle down class," said the teacher. She gave each of us a question paper, an answer paper and a sharp pencil. The teacher said, "You have 30 minutes for the test and the time starts now."
42. Our cats sleep on my bed.
43. My friends are moving house.
44. The roads were very busy.
45. My brothers play ice hockey.

46. The teachers collect our books each Friday.
47–54. Possible answers include:
47. partnership
48. unusual
49. musical
50. comfortable
51. freedom
52. decorative
53. fortunate
54. curiosity
55. dance
56. notebook
57. they
58. Paris
59. massive
60. silently
61. blue
62. pink
63. green
64. red
65–66. tone, stable
67–68. were, shame
69–70. cold, shout

Paper 10
1. Martin
2. miner
3. heart
4. Someone who keeps going to work while other people are on strike.
5. Because his father is not on strike but their fathers are.
6. Because strikers did not get any money from the Government and had to survive on donations.
7–8. Robbie doesn't tell his mum about his problems at school, and his mum doesn't tell his dad that the shopkeeper wouldn't serve her.
9. Because they are trying to protect each other from the extra worry.
10. The neighbour's baby, who is younger than Katy, is bigger and crawling but Katy stays still as if she is just trying to stay alive.
11. Because they are very worried about Katy and just concentrate on how she is, one day at a time.
12. He thinks that his father is afraid that Katy won't get better and wants to make sure she will not be cold during the winter.
13. antisocial
14. unusual
15. unreasonable
16. disloyalty
17. impractical
18. inaccurate
19. disapprove
20. unfashionable
21–25. The boys grabbed his pack lunches and raced out of the door. They shouted a hasty goodbye up the stairs to their mother and he reminded them to be back by lunchtime.
When the boys got to the canal we set up their fishing rods. Tim's rod jerked almost immediately and she began to reel it in. On the hook was a rusty tin can, covered in water weed. Tim looked at Lewis and us both laughed.
26–30. Possible answers include:
26. If I don't eat something soon, my stomach will rumble.
27. I might find my missing book if I tidy my room.
28. Had we known it was going to rain, we would have stayed inside.
29. If Daniel calls for me, please tell him I'm at the park.
30. Should I be late home, Mum will worry.
31. A new postman delivered a parcel.
32. Dad burnt the toast and set the smoke alarm off.
33. The blue team won the quiz.
34. The teacher set the test.
35. The gale blew some branches off the trees.
36. The scary film frightened many people.
37–42. Possible answers include:
37. The sea was a roaring monster.
38. The sun was a fiery ball.
39. The carnival was a riot of colour.
40. The snow was a soft blanket.
41. The waterfall was a wall of shimmering water.
42. The road was a serpent, winding between the hills.
43–48. Possible answers include:
43. Anna decided to catch the bus as the trains were all delayed.
44. The class played basketball after lunch while the teachers were in their meeting.
45. Lying in the gutter, the boys found a wallet.

46. When they got hot, the girls stopped and bought an ice cream.
47. There was a full moon, although it was covered by thick clouds.
48. The door was locked when I got home.
49–56. Possible answers include:
49–50. patter   plop
51–52. chattering   howling
53–54. splashing   drip
55–56. whoosh   chug
57. There is no point in being upset over things that have already happened.
58. If lots of people help, it is easier to get things done.
59. You should take responsibility for your own mistakes, rather than blaming something else.
60. It doesn't matter how strong a group is, if there is one weak person in it, the group will not be strong.
61. We always think that what other people have is better than what we have.
62. If two people think about a problem, the solution will be easier to find.
63–70. Possible answers include:
63. painfully
64. thickly
65. finally
66. dangerously
67. completely
68. brightly
69. gratefully
70. timidly

Paper 11
1. King Aegeus
2. 13
3. Naxos
4. long-running dispute or argument
5. Answers may vary, but could include: No, because he didn't want him to go in the first place, suggesting that he thought he would fail to kill the minotaur.
6. He planned to use a white sail, which could be seen from Athens while his boat was still out at sea.
7. a maze
8. Because if the minotaur was lost in the labyrinth, it would be less likely to escape.
9. It helps him because he ties one end to the door and unravels it as he goes, so he can follow it back to the entrance later.
10. Answers may vary, but could include: No, because she gives him the sword he uses to kill the minotaur and the string he uses to find his way back out of the labyrinth.
11. Because he had promised to take her with him and he was breaking this promise.
12. He thought that Theseus was dead when he saw the black sail and in his grief he jumped to his death.
13. cocoa
14. ghost
15. rhyme
16. leopard
17. answer
18. raspberry
19. lamb
20. guitar
21–35. We crept through the forest, looking carefully about us. "Look, there's one!" said Dad. We looked up and saw a red squirrel in the branches above us. It looked at us for a moment then leapt into another tree and disappeared from view.
36. United Kingdom
37. European Union
38. as soon as possible
39. for example
40. Member of Parliament
41. for your information
42. The theatre is near here.
43. I have to be back before it gets dark.
44. We will have enough time to finish our work.
45. We can have fish and chips for tea.
46. We should tidy up now.
47. It is going to be sunny today.
48–50. find: to locate
fined: made to pay a fee for breaking a rule
51–53. real: genuine
reel: a spool or roll of thread or line
54–56. peer: to look closely
pier: a structure built out over the sea
57–62. Possible answers include:
57. asked
58. replied
59. demanded
60. complained

61. argued
62. whispered
63–70. Possible answers include:
63–64. within, without
65–66. forehead, forecast
67–68. international, interview
69–70. understand, understated

Paper 12
1. Burma
2. 1995
3. 54
4. Because they are strong and specially adapted to moving around that terrain and can get to places the vehicles could not, especially if roads have been damaged.
5. Because they wanted to support their country in the war.
6–7. searching for wounded, locating explosives
8. They could reach places that vehicles could not.
9. Because they were sometimes the only reliable way to get messages behind enemy lines.
10. If their planes crashed or ditched, the pigeons could be sent back with details of the crew's location, so they could be rescued.
11–12. Arguments will vary.

13–14. pin   pit   hit   him
15–16. man   mat   met   get
17–18. pet   set   sat   sap
19–20. hot   cot   cat   can
21–26. Possible answers include:
21. fingers
22. bonbons
23. perfect
24. trees
25. pelted
26. silently
27. furthermore, moreover
28. nevertheless, however
29. therefore, consequently
30. because, as
31. in contrast, on the other hand
32. margarine
33. benefit
34. grammar
35. miniature
36. parliament
37. vegetable
38. journalist
39. signature
40. tension
41. confusion
42. magician
43. politician
44. attention
45. direction
46. electrician
47. explosion
48. fiction
Formal language: 49, 51, 53, 54
Informal language: 50, 52
55. true
56. false
57. true
58. false
59–62. Answers will vary.
63–70. Possible answers include:
63. pig
64. towards
65. skip
66. we
67. sleepily
68. because
69. smelly
70. butterfly

Paper 13
1. Hind Street
2. twice
3. silver
4. The shop would have been opened earlier and the rings and bracelets would also have been taken out of the safe.
5. Because they were still locked in the safe.
6. Someone who is involved in a crime with someone else.
7. Lizzie Butler would have felt very frightened during the robbery because men were armed and might have hurt her.
8. It had distinctive French number plates.
9–10. It might still be somewhere in the town, or it could have left the town along the B154 Bisham Road.
11. They think they might try to sell it.

12. By offering a community award.
13. herd
14. choir
15. pod
16. clutch
17. colony
18. company
19. warren
20. quiver
21–26. Possible answers include:
21. While
22. but
23. when
24. Until
25. so
26. Although
27. the children's toys
28. the three boys' houses
29. a witch's hat
30. the people's bags
31. the men's newspapers
32. the tree's trunk
33–40. Possible answers include:
33. for
34. before
35. to
36. with
37. on
38. for
39. at
40. at
41–46. Arguments will vary.
47–52. megabyte, soap opera, memory stick, wind farm, carbon footprint
53–60. Answers might include:
53. dough
54. plead
55. sour
56. treat
57. tried
58. weight
59. heard
60. stable
61. simile
62. simile
63. metaphor
64. metaphor
65. Oliver ate the crunchy (apple).
66. The girls read their (books) quietly.
67. I don't like (arguments).
68. The team won their (match).
69. We have a new (car).
70. Amy could not find her (shoes).

Paper 14
1. 58 years
2. grey
3. his father
4. change
5. his house
6. Local removals companies
7. Because he had moved so often as a child that he was tired of it.
8. She loved interior design and hoped that he would be like his father and keep moving house, to give her lots of new interiors to work on.
9. Because she couldn't have real houses to decorate and had begun to go a little mad.
10. boredom
11. Because his grandmother was rather frail and nobody could understand how she had produced so many fine houses.
12. How his father lost his fortune.
13. snowflake
14. motorbike
15. rainbow
16. farmyard
17. blackberry
18. pigtail
19. notebook
20. grapefruit
21. postbox
22. iceberg
23. damaged
24. sopping
25. worried
26. hungry
27. naughty
28. scamper
29. pause
30. clunk
31–36. Sentences will vary.
37. cellos
38. volcanoes
39. discos
40. radios
41. echoes

42. dominoes
43. solos
44. flamingos
45. heroes
46. kangaroos
47–52. Answers will vary.
53. examination
54. approval
55. enjoyment
56. discovery
57. medication
58. delivery
59. extension
60. repetition
61. a spherical object
62. a formal dance
63. a supporter of a band or team
64. a device that moves air to provide a cooling effect
65. a valve used to control the flow of water
66. to knock something gently
67. pineapple
68. grapefruit
69. apricot
70. banana

Paper 15
1. windows
2. wolf
3. a million
4. a huge rush of animals or people in the same direction
5. storm clouds
6. The windows are not crying. The tears are rain drops streaming down the glass.
7. The first verse describes how powerful the storm is and the damage it can do. The second verse is calmer and describes how the storm passes.
8–9. 'stealing timber and tiles', 'slapped'
10. 'like errant guard dogs'
11. 'bellow and bully'/ 'teem with tears'
12. raindrops left on the trees
13. PM
14. RSCPA
15. mm
16. www
17. CD
18. Jan
19. NY
20. UN
21–33. "You'll never believe what I've just seen!" giggled Chloe.
"What?" asked Megan. "Tell me quickly!"
34. vandalise
35. pollinate
36. classify
37. vocalise
38. apologise
39. medicate
40. notify
41. When she was on holiday, my aunt fell ill.
42. Until it stopped raining, we stood under the bridge.
43. After the fire bell rang, we left the classroom quickly.
44. Before it could escape, I closed the rabbit's cage.
45. So she could see where she was going, she put the light on.
46. Although it was cloudy, we decided to have the picnic.
47–54. Added words will vary.
prescribe, prescription, presentable, president, pressure, presume, pretence
55–60. Possible answers include:
55. cold, green
56. huge, black
57. wet mud
58. Fragrant pink
59. delicious, spicy
60. Bright, colourful
61–62. cease, strain
63–64. grin, steam
65–66. boat, platter
67–68. a small, long-tailed rodent; hand-operated device for controlling a computer
69–70. a small book on plain or lined paper for writing in; a laptop computer

4

PAPER 9

If there was one thing we loved in 6C, it was having a supply teacher. There was   1
something delicious about ruining their lessons a bit at a time. The disappointing ones
crumbled by morning break and, after a stiff talking-to from the head teacher, we'd be
doing colouring in and handwriting practice in silence for the rest of the day. The best
ones had a bit of fight in them, providing us with entertainment until lunchtime at least.   5
Either way we would always end up doing handwriting and colouring.

This one, in particular, looked like she was going to be a pushover. Neat and tidy
Miss Smith, our usual class teacher, had conquered us over the past two terms with a
combination of zero tolerance of mischief-making and ruthless efficiency. Her lessons
were planned with military precision. Handouts for the entire week were colour-coded   10
and laid out in regiments on her desk. Completed the work early? No problem, try pink
worksheet 3.2. Work too easy? Green 2.8. Too hard? Beige 1.2. Whatever your excuse
for not working, Miss Smith could put her hand on the solution in a heartbeat.

The same could not be said of today's cover teacher, Miss Mess. Across the desk,
and most other horizontal surfaces in the room, were higgledy-piggledy piles of   15
Miss Smith's precious worksheets stacked, it appeared, in random order.

We took one look at the chaos and smiled. With Miss Smith's worksheet system out
of action, Miss Mess would have to rely on a zero-tolerance policy on behaviour.
In her tent dress and comfy shoes, she really didn't look the type to pull it off.

"Good morning, 6C," said Miss Mess in a small, feeble voice. "Please sit down."   20

The class remained standing, waiting to see what she would do next. We were in for a
surprise.

"I said, sit down 6C," said Miss Mess, more forcefully, fixing the class with a curious,
powerful stare.

The better-mannered children in 6C took their seats. The rest of us began to experience   25
a strange sensation behind the knees. It began with a tingle that became numbness
and then a distinct weakness. Several of us had the good sense to sit down before our
legs collapsed beneath them. A few continued in their defiance and ended up
wriggling on the floor like slugs.

Miss Mess, it seemed, would be no pushover.   30

Circle your answers.

1. What is the name of Class 6C's usual teacher?

Miss Brown   Miss Smith   Miss Mess

2. How long has she been teaching the class?

> two months   two terms   two years

3. Which worksheet would the children in 6C be given if they found the work too easy?

> green 3.2   green 2.8   beige 3.2

Answer these questions.

4. What did 6C like best about having a supply teacher?

_____

5. What does the word *delicious* (line 2) tell us about how the children feel when they tease the cover teacher?

_____

6–7. What two things would 6C always end up doing, when they had a cover teacher?

_____   _____

8–9. Find two war-type phrases which suggest that Miss Smith has had to battle with 6C.

_____

_____

10. Why might the contrast in how the teachers look affect how the children behave for Miss Mess?

_____

11. What does the word *horizontal* (line 15) mean?

_____

12. Do you think Miss Mess is like the other cover teachers the children have had? Explain your answer.

_____   /12

Add *did* or *done* to complete each sentence.

13. I _____ my homework before I watched TV.

14. When the window was broken, the girls admitted they had _____ it.

15–16. I _____ not do the washing up because I thought my sister had _____ it.

17–18. When I saw the picture that Chris had _____, I _____ one just like it.

/6

Combine one word from each column to write eight **compound words**.

grass   fall
pepper   shell
gold   hive
sun   hopper
egg   barrow
wheel   fish
water   mint
bee   shine

19. _____   **20.** _____

21. _____   **22.** _____

23. _____   **24.** _____

25. _____   **26.** _____

/8

27–41. Write this passage again, adding the capital letters and punctuation.

settle down class said the teacher she gave each of us a question paper an answer paper and a sharp pencil the teacher said you have 30 minutes for the test and the time starts now

_____

_____

_____

_____

/15

Write these sentences again, changing the **nouns** and **verbs** to their **plural** form.

42. Our cat sleeps on my bed.

_____

43. My friend is moving house.

_____

44. The road was very busy.

_____

45. My brother plays ice hockey.

_____

46. The teacher collects our books each Friday.

_____   /5

Add a **prefix** or **suffix** to each **root word** to make a new word. Remember to make any necessary changes to spelling.

47. partner _____   **48.** usual _____

49. music _____   **50.** comfort _____

51. free _____   **52.** decorate _____

53. fortune _____   **54.** curious _____   /8

Choose a word from the box to match each of these word types.

they   massive   dance   Paris   silently   notebook

55. verb _____   **56.** noun _____

57. pronoun _____   **58.** proper noun _____

59. adjective _____   **60.** adverb _____   /6

Add the name of a colour to complete each common phrase.

61. out of the _____   **62.** in the _____

63. pea _____ with envy   **64.** _____ letter day

/4

Move a letter from one word to the other in each pair to make two new words, then write down both new words.

e.g. fleet	fat	*feet*	*flat*
65–66. stone	table	_____	_____
67–68. where	same	_____	_____
69–70. could	shot	_____	_____

/6

/70

PAPER 10

In 1984, government plans to close several coal mines caused a national miner's strike.   1
Because of the way the strike was organised, miners and their families received no
benefits from the government and had to survive on donations of money and food from
supporters across the country. Robbie, whose father was a miner, lived in Yorkshire.

3rd July 1984   5

Today was Martin's birthday. He had a party after school but of course I wasn't invited.
Who'd want a scab at their party? It is getting harder and harder to go to school. I sit
on my own most of the time in class, unless Miss Carter makes someone sit with me
but even then they make sure their stuff doesn't touch mine, like I've got the plague or
something. Someone put mud in my lunchbox last week so now I have to stay in the   10
classroom at break and lunchtime.

Mum asked me if everything is OK at school and I told her it was. She has enough to worry about already. The doctor says that Katy will have to have another operation on her heart soon. Our neighbour's baby, who was born two weeks after Katy, is already much bigger than she is and crawling too. Katy just lies there most of the time, like she is concentrating on just staying alive. I can tell Mum is worried sick about her. About other things too. The man in Studley's refused to serve us when we went in to buy bread yesterday. Said he was sorry but he couldn't take money from us, not when other people were going hungry. Mum made me promise not to tell Dad about it. He would be furious if he knew. 15

20

Mum says we should be proud of what Dad is doing but it's hard. If he was striking like the others everything would be easier. I hate the things people are saying about us but I can understand why they are angry. They are thinking about the future, about things that might happen six months or a year from now. We haven't thought that way since Katy was born. Dad is just worried about being able to pay to keep the house warm for Katy this winter. He would never admit it but he is just as scared as the rest of us. 25

Circle your answers.

1. Whose birthday was it?

Miss Carter   Robbie   Martin

2. What job did Robbie's father do?

miner   teacher   shopkeeper

3. What part of Katy's body does the doctor says will need to be operated on?

brain   lungs   heart

4. What is the meaning of the word *scab* (line 7), as it is used in the text?

_____

_____

5. Why do you think the children at school are being so unkind to Robbie?

_____

_____

6. Why are some people going hungry? (line 19)

_____

_____

7–8. Find two secrets that people in Robbie's family keep from each other.

_____

_____

9. Why do you think Robbie's family are keeping secrets from each other?

_____

10. Find some evidence in the text that shows how weak Katy is.

_____

_____

11. Why do you think Robbie's family are not thinking six months or a year ahead, like other people are?

_____

_____

12. How does Robbie explain what his father is doing?

_____

_____ /12

Add a **prefix** to each word to make its **antonym**.

13. _____ social   **14.** _____ usual

15. _____ reasonable   **16.** _____ loyalty

17. _____ practical   **18.** _____ accurate

19. _____ approve   **20.** _____ fashionable   /8

21–25. Find and underline five pronoun errors in this piece of text.

The boys grabbed his pack lunches and raced out of the door. They shouted a hasty goodbye up the stairs to their mother and he reminded them to be back by lunchtime.

When the boys got to the canal we set up their fishing rods. Tim's rod jerked almost immediately and she began to reel it in. On the hook was a rusty tin can, covered in water weed. Tim looked at Lewis and us both laughed.

/5

Complete these sentences in a suitable way.

26. If I don't eat something soon, _____.

27. _____ if I tidy my room.

28. Had we known it was going to rain, _____.

29. If Daniel calls for me _____.

30. Should I be late home, _____.

/5

Write these sentences again, using **active verbs**.

31. A parcel was delivered by a new postman.

_____

32. The smoke alarm was set off when Dad burnt the toast.

_____

33. The quiz was won by the blue team.

_____

34. The test was set by the teacher.

_____

35. Some branches were blown off the trees by the gale.

_____

36. Many people were frightened by the scary film.

_____

/6

Write a suitable metaphor to describe each thing.

37. the sea _____

38. the sun _____

39. a carnival _____

40. snow _____

41. a waterfall _____

42. a road _____ /6

Add a **subordinate clause** to each **main clause**.

43. Anna decided to catch the bus, _____.

44. The class played basketball after lunch, _____.

45. _____, the boy found a wallet.

46. _____, the girls stopped and bought an ice cream.

47. There was a full moon, _____.

48. The door was locked, _____. /6

Write two onomatopoeic words that could be used to describe each thing.

49–50. rainfall _____ _____

51–52. monkeys _____ _____

53–54. a swimming pool _____ _____

55–56. a steam train _____ _____ /8

Write a sentence to explain what each proverb means.

57. Don't cry over spilt milk.

_____

58. Many hands make light work.

_____

59. A bad workman blames his tools.

_____

60. A chain is only as strong as its weakest link.

_____

61. The grass is always greener on the other side.

_____

62. Two heads are better than one.

_____ /6

Think of a suitable **adverb** to complete each sentence.

63. The old lady hobbled _____ down the road.

64. By the morning, snow lay _____ over everything.

65. When we _____ arrived, all the best seats had been taken.

66. The little boy was standing _____ close to the edge of the cliff.

67. At the end of the race, the runners were _____ exhausted.

68. I love to wear _____ coloured clothes.

69. The thirsty girl _____ took the glass of cold water.

70. The little boy _____ approached the big dog. /8

/70

Theseus and the Minotaur

Long ago, a feud raged between King Minos of Crete and King Aegeus of Athens.   1
The son of Minos had been attacked and killed in Athens and, despite his best efforts,
Aegeus had been unable to find the culprits. Eventually, Aegeus had to agree to hand
over seven young men and seven young women to Minos every seven years. These
people were taken to Crete where they were fed to the minotaur, a fearsome beast   5
which was imprisoned in a labyrinth beneath the palace.

The son of Aegeus, who was called Theseus, was unhappy with the deal that had
been struck. He begged his father to allow him to be one of the seven young men sent
to Crete and promised that once there he would kill the minotaur. Aegeus reluctantly
agreed, and Theseus prepared to set sail for Crete, with the 13 other young men and   10
women who were to enter the labyrinth. He told his father that, if he was successful,
he would use a white sail on the return voyage, so that Athens would know of his
victory all the sooner.

When the boat arrived at Crete, King Minos was waiting for them with his daughter
Ariadne, who took one look at Theseus and fell in love with him. Later that night, she   15
crept to the cell he was being held in. Giving him a ball of thread, she told him to tie it
to the door of the labyrinth and let it unravel as he moved through the passages, so that
he would be able to find his way back to the entrance. She also gave him a powerful
sword with which to slay the minotaur. In return, she made him promise to take her
with him when he left Crete.   20

The next morning, the young Athenians were taken to the labyrinth and shut inside.
Leaving the others at the entrance, Theseus tied the thread to the door and went alone
into the maze of passages. Some time later he heard the minotaur moving in the
darkness ahead of him. He rounded a corner and there it was, huge and powerful,
with the body of a man and the head of a bull. Theseus and the minotaur fought   25
furiously but eventually Theseus managed to slay the beast and find his way back
out of the labyrinth.

True to his word, Theseus took Ariadne with him when he left Crete, but he soon tired
of her and left her on the island of Naxos. This angered the gods, who punished
Theseus by making him forget to use a white sail on the voyage back to Athens.   30
Seeing a black sail, Aegeus assumed that Theseus had been killed by the minotaur
and in his grief he threw himself into the sea and died. Theseus became king, but
never forgave himself for causing his father's death.

Circle your answers.

1. Who was Theseus the son of?

   King Midas   King Minos   King Aegeus

2. How many young people travelled to Crete with Theseus?

   7   14   13

3. Where did Theseus leave Ariadne?

   Athens   Naxos   Crete

Answer these questions.

4. What is the meaning of the word *feud* (line 1)?

   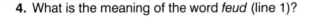

5. Do you think Aegeus was confident that Theseus would kill the minotaur?
   Give a reason for your answer.

   _____

6. How did Theseus plan to get news of his safety to his father as quickly as possible?

   _____

7. What is a labyrinth?

   _____

8. Why would a labyrinth be a good place to imprison a beast as terrible as the minotaur?

   _____

9. Explain how the ball of thread helps Theseus in the labyrinth.

   _____

10. Do you think Theseus would have been able to slay the minotaur without Ariadne's help?
    Use evidence from the text to back up your answer.

    _____

    _____

11. Why were the gods angry when Theseus left Ariadne on the island?

_____

12. What was the effect of the god's punishment on Aegeus?

_____

_____ /12

> Write these words again, adding the missing silent letter.

13. coco _____ **14.** gost _____

15. ryme _____ **16.** lepard _____

17. anser _____ **18.** rasberry _____

19. lam _____ **20.** gitar _____ /8

21–35. Write this passage again, separating the words and adding capital letters and punctuation.

wecreptthroughtheforestlookingcarefullyaboutuslooktheresonesaiddadwelookedup
andsawaredsquirrelinthebranchesaboveusitlookedatusforamomentthenleaptinto
anothertree

_____

_____

_____

_____

_____ /15

> Write down what each abbreviation means.

36. UK _____

37. EU _____

38. asap _____

39. e.g. _____

40. MP _____

41. fyi _____   /6

Write these questions again, as statements.

42. Is the theatre near here?

_____

43. Do I have to be back before it gets dark?

_____

44. Will we have enough time to finish our work?

_____

45. Can we have fish and chips for tea?

_____

46. Should we tidy up now?

_____

47. Is it going to be sunny today?

_____   /6

Write a homophone for each word, then write a short definition for both words.

48–50. find   _____

_____   _____

51–53. real   _____

_____   _____

54–56. peer   _____

_____   _____   /9

Use a different **synonym** for the word *said* to complete each sentence.

57. "Are you going to drama club tonight?" _____ Beth.

58. "No, it's on Friday this week," _____ Susie.

59. "Be quiet immediately!" _____ Mr Andrews.

60. Martin _____ , "This soup is cold."

61. "That's not yours, it's mine," _____ Mandy.

62. Ryan _____ , "Be very quiet or they'll hear us."

/6

Write down two words that start with each **prefix**.

63–64. with _____ _____

65–66. fore _____ _____

67–68. inter _____ _____

69–70. under _____ _____

/8

/70

PAPER 12

When we think about the First and Second World Wars, we tend to think about the people who were fighting, or what it was like for those left behind at home. Behind the scenes, however, hundreds of thousands of animals risked their lives to support the war effort, showing such bravery that many were later awarded medals.

Around 16 million animals served in the First World War, including mules, horses, elephants and camels. Many were used to transport troops and equipment across a variety of difficult terrains. Dogs were also used to carry messages from trench to trench when telephone wires were damaged by shellfire. They wore metal canisters attached to their collars to store the messages and were able to cover rough, broken ground much more quickly than a man could. Initially only stray dogs were used, but as the war dragged on, more than 7,000 people offered their pet dogs for training.

During World War Two, dogs were even trained as paradogs, being parachuted with their handlers into enemy territory where they helped to track and attack the enemy and sniff out mines and other hidden explosives. One dog, Rob, made 22 parachute drops. Dogs were also used both in Britain and behind enemy lines to search for the wounded after bombing raids.

In Burma, elephants were used to help build bridges and to move aircraft and other heavy machinery. They were perfect for the job, being both very strong and able to reach remote parts of the jungle that no vehicle could.

Pigeons were used to carry messages in both World Wars with around half a million birds being used. Although communications technology had improved by the Second World War, pigeons were often the only reliable way to get messages behind enemy lines.

As well as carrying messages, the birds were routinely carried by RAF aircrews during the Second World War, so that if the plane crashed or ditched in the sea, the birds could fly back to Britain carrying details of the crew's location. Around 20,000 pigeons died while carrying out their duties and pigeons received more medals for bravery than any other species. They were such effective messengers that the Swiss army continued to use them until 1995.

The medal awarded to animals is the Dickin Medal, also known as the Animals' Victoria Cross. The medal was named after Maria Dickin, who founded animal charity PDSA. Between 1943 and 1949, medals were awarded to 54 animals who displayed outstanding bravery, including 32 pigeons. The other medals were awarded to 18 dogs, three horses and a cat.

A monument in London is dedicated to the bravery of animals in war. The script reads as follows: "To all the animals that served and died alongside British and Allied forces in wars and campaigns throughout time. They had no choice."

Circle your answers.

1. Where were elephants used during World War Two?

India   Burma   Africa

2. When did the Swiss army stop using pigeons to carry messages?

1943   1949   1995

3. How many Dickin Medals were awarded between 1943 and 1949.

54   45   18

Answer these questions.

4. Why might animals like mules and camels sometimes be better at transporting troops and equipment than trucks?

_____

5. Why do you think people offered their pet dogs for use in the trenches?

_____

6–7. Find two jobs that dogs did during World War Two.

_____

_____

8. Why were elephants so useful in the Burmese jungle?

_____

_____

9. Why were pigeons still used to carry messages during the Second World War, despite improvements in communications technology?

_____

_____

10. What was the benefit for RAF crews carrying pigeons?

_____

_____

11–12. The script on the monument in London says that animals that die in wars have no choice. Is it fair to use animals in this way? Write one argument in favour of using animals like this and one argument against.

_____

_____

_____ /12

Complete the word chain by changing one letter at a time.

	e.g.	ear	eat	fat	cat

13–14.	pin	_____	_____	him

15–16.	man	_____	_____	get

17–18.	pet	_____	_____	sap

19–20.	hot	_____	_____	can

/8

Complete each sentence with a suitable **alliterative** word.

21. The cold pinched our cheeks with frost fringed _____.

22. The shop was crowded with people buying boxes of _____.

23. My Gran's peach pies are _____.

24. The bird soared over the tops of the tallest _____.

25. I tried to stand up on my ice skates while people _____ past me.

26. The children sat _____ in school.

/6

Draw lines to join up the pairs of **connectives** with similar meanings.

27.	furthermore	on the other hand
28.	nevertheless	as
29.	therefore	however
30.	because	moreover
31.	in contrast	consequently

/5

Add the missing unstressed vowel to each word.

32. marg__rine

33. ben__fit

34. gramm__r

35. mini__ture

36. parli___ment

37. veg___table

38. journ___list

39. sign___ture

/8

Add the **suffix** *cian*, *sion* or *tion* to complete each word.

40. ten_____

41. confu_____

42. magi_____

43. politi_____

44. atten_____

45. direc_____

46. electri_____

47. explo_____

48. fic_____

/9

Put a tick by each sentence that uses formal language and a cross by those that do not.

49. Children are not permitted on school property between the hours of 4.30pm and 8.45am.

50. Let's go bowling after school.

51. Your bank account has been credited with the agreed funds.

52. Thanks for the great present!

53. Parking is prohibited.

54. A valid licence and permit must be held in order to fish in this river.

/6

Read the passage, then write true or false by each statement.

The school lies to the south of Kate's house. To the east of the school is the park and to the west of the school is the library. Due south of the school is the swimming pool.

55. The school is between Kate's house and the swimming pool. _____

56. The park is to the north west of Kate's house. _____

57. Of all of the places mentioned, the swimming pool is the furthest south. _____

58. If you walked directly from the park to the library you would walk right past the swimming pool. _____

/4

Write an **adjectival phrase** to describe each thing.

59. a balloon _____

60. a spider _____

61. a test _____

62. ice cream _____ /4

Write down an example of each word type.

63. noun _____ **64.** preposition _____

65. verb _____ **66.** pronoun _____

67. adverb _____ **68.** conjunction _____

69. adjective _____ **70.** compound word _____ /8

/70

PAPER 13

Local jewellers in double robbery

Police are appealing for witnesses to come forward after a town centre jewellers   1
was robbed for the second time in just six weeks. Marley's Jewellers, in Hind Street,
was targeted on Thursday as staff arrived for work in the morning. Thieves stole
watches and gold chains to the value of around £13,000, but store manager
Gerald Marley says that it could have been much worse.   5

"We were late opening the shop that day because I got held up in the road works on
the by-pass. Normally by that time all of the rings and bracelets would have been out
of the safe. As it was, we had only had time to get out the watches and some of the
gold chains."

Two men, who are believed to have been armed, burst into the shop at 9.45 on   10
Thursday morning as Mr Marley and shop assistant Lizzy Butler were arranging the
displays of watches and chains. The robbers' faces were partially covered but they
were both white with brown hair. One was tall with a slim build, the other short and
stockily built. The taller man threatened Miss Butler while his accomplice grabbed
handfuls of jewellery and stuffed it into the pockets of a black leather jacket.   15

Police believe there was a further man waiting in a getaway car behind the shop in
Bridge Street. The car, a silver estate with distinctive French number plates, was spotted
speeding off down Hind Street, but what happened to it after that remains a mystery.

Chief Inspector Rob Day explains, "Mr Marley raised the alarm as soon as the thieves
had left the store and we immediately alerted all of our patrols to be on the look out   20
for the car. If the thieves had made their escape along the by-pass, they would have
been seen by one of the police patrols who were controlling the queues of traffic.
It seems most likely that if they left the town at all, it would have been via the B154
Bisham Road. However, we are not ruling out the possibility that the thieves live in the
town, especially since they were, we believe, the same men involved in another   25
robbery at the store on the 12th May."

"This was obviously a very serious attack and although fortunately nobody was hurt,
both Mr Marley and Miss Butler are clearly very shaken up. We are very keen to catch
these men before they have the chance to strike again."

Anyone who saw a silver estate car in the Hind Street area of the town on Thursday   30
morning, or has seen it since, is asked to contact the police station. Similarly, the
police are asking for people to get in touch if they are offered watches or chains to buy
under suspicious circumstances. There is a community award for information
leading to the conviction of the thieves.

Circle your answers.

1. On what street is Marley's Jewellers?

   Bridge Street   Hind Street   the by-pass

2. How many times has the jewellers been robbed?

   twice   once   six times

3. What colour was the getaway car?

   black   blue   silver

Answer these questions.

4. Why would the robbery have been worse if it had taken place on any other day?

_____

5. Why didn't the thieves take any rings or bracelets?

_____

6. What is the meaning of the word *accomplice* (line 14)?

_____

7. Write a sentence describing how you think Lizzie Butler would have felt during the robbery.

_____

8. What was unusual about the appearance of the car that witnesses may have noticed?

_____

9–10. What two things do the police think might have happened to the car after it was seen speeding away down Hind Street?

_____

_____

11. What do the police think that the thieves might try to do with the stolen jewellery?

_____

12. How do the police hope to encourage people to come forward with information?

_____   /12

Pick a word to complete each **collective noun**.

choir   company   herd   quiver   pod   warren   clutch   colony

13. a _____ of elephants   14. a _____ of singers

15. a _____ of whales   16. a _____ of eggs

17. a _____ of ants   **18.** a _____ of actors

19. a _____ of rabbits   **20.** a _____ of arrows   /8

Add a suitable **conjunction** to complete each sentence.

21. _____ I finished my homework, my brother watched TV.

22. I enjoy gymnastics _____ Paul prefers hockey.

23. It was funny _____ the clown threw the custard pie.

24. _____ I can buy a new bag, I have to use my old one.

25. The hotel had a great swimming pool _____ we spent a lot of time there.

26. _____ my brother is younger than me, he is taller.   /6

Circle the correct use of the **apostrophe**.

27. the children's toys   the childrens' toys

28. the three boy's houses   the three boys' houses

29. a witch's hat   a witches' hat

30. the peoples' bags   the people's bags

31. the mens' newspapers   the men's newspapers

32. the trees' trunk   the tree's trunk   /6

Use a suitable **preposition** to complete each sentence.

33. An exciting-looking parcel came _____ me this morning.

34. Jacob won't be back _____ teatime.

35. Claire told the secret _____ her friend.

36. Dad mended the broken vase _____ strong glue.

37. Rebecca spent all of her pocket money _____ sweets.

38. Eating lots of fruit and vegetables is very good _____ you.

39. My brother is really good _____ skateboarding.

40. The party starts _____ 4.30pm.

/8

Write a short balanced argument about whether eating fried food is a good idea, using these words and phrases.

41–46.   however   furthermore   in contrast   in addition

                  although   in conclusion

_____

_____

_____

_____

_____

_____

_____

/6

Circle the words and phrases that have entered the English language in the past 100 years.

47–52. megabyte   soap opera   field   pan

        memory stick   plough   iron   castle

        wind farm   windmill   journal   carbon footprint

/6

Write down a word with the same bold letter string as each word, but a different pronunciation.

53. c**ough**   _____   **54.** br**ead**   _____

55. hon**our**   _____   **56.** sw**ea**t   _____

57. p**ie**ce   _____   **58.** he**ight**   _____

59. f**ear**   _____   **60.** miser**able** _____

/8

Write **simile** or **metaphor** beside each phrase.

61. He is as gentle as a lamb. _____

62. She had hair like spun gold. _____

63. My cousins are little devils. _____

64. The moon was a pale balloon in the sky. _____   /4

Underline the **subject** and circle the **object** of each sentence.

65. Oliver ate the crunchy apple.

66. The girls read their books quietly.

67. I don't like arguments.

68. The team won their match.

69. We have a new car.

70. Amy could not find her shoes.   /6

/70

PAPER 14

Like a great many Victorians, my great-grandfather believed that change was a good thing. We know this because in the course of his adult life he lived in a total of 28 different houses, believing that so much buying and selling of property must surely make him wealthy. He never became rich, but several local removals companies did.

Having been uprooted regularly throughout his childhood, his son, my grandfather, took a very different view. After marrying my grandmother, in an ill-fitting grey suit, he bought a house and there they lived for the next 58 years until he died and was buried, in the same grey suit. He never became rich either.

All of this was very unfortunate for my grandmother, who loved designing and decorating the interiors of houses and had married my grandfather hoping he would follow in his father's footsteps. She eventually went a little mad and began building and decorating dolls' houses, because she couldn't have the real thing.

Everyone saw it as a hobby, but when she died (of boredom, most likely) my father discovered no fewer than 220 beautiful dolls' houses hidden in her attic. Nobody could understand how one rather frail old lady had managed to produce so many beautiful dolls' houses.

In any case, the houses were so finely made that they turned out to be very valuable. Many were sold off to entertain the children of wealthy people all over the world. The rest can be found in museums and private collections. And that is how my father eventually became rich. But it is how he lost his fortune that really concerns us in this story.

Circle your answers.

1. For how many years did the narrator's grandparents live in the same house?

    28   220   58

2. What colour was the suit the narrator's grandfather was married in?

    grey   blue   brown

3. Which member of the narrator's family eventually became rich?

    his great grandfather   his father   his grandfather

Answer these questions.

4. What did many Victorian people think was a good thing, according to the text?

    _____

5. What did the narrator's great-grandfather keep changing?

    _____

6. Who made money out of his habit?

    _____

7. Why does the narrator suggest that his grandfather stayed in the same house for so long?

    _____

8. What reason is suggested for why the narrator's grandmother married the man she did?

_____

9. Why did she start to build and decorate doll's houses?

_____

10. What does the writer suggest killed his grandmother?

_____

11. Why was the number and quality of the doll's houses surprising?

_____

12. According to the narrator, what is the story really about?

_____   /12

Use one word from each column to make ten **compound words**.

snow	bow
motor	berg
rain	berry
farm	bike
black	tail
pig	book
note	fruit
grape	yard
post	flake
ice	box

13. _____   **14.** _____

15. _____   **16.** _____

17. _____   **18.** _____

19. _____   **20.** _____

21. _____   **22.** _____   /10

Circle the best **synonym** for each word?

23. **cracked**	damaged	destroyed
24. **saturated**	damp	sopping
25. **concerned**	desperate	worried
26. **peckish**	starving	hungry
27. **mischievous**	evil	naughty
28. **scurry**	scamper	crawl
29. **hesitate**	pause	stop
30. **click**	clunk	shatter

/8

Write a sentence using each of these **adverbs**.

31. foolishly

_____

32. heroically

_____

33. carelessly

_____

34. greatly

_____

35. clearly

_____

36. gently

_____

/6

Write the plural for each noun.

37. cello _____ **38.** volcano _____

39. disco _____ **40.** radio _____

41. echo _____ **42.** domino _____

43. solo _____ **44.** flamingo _____

45. hero _____ **46.** kangaroo _____   /10

Write a sentence containing **personification** to describe each thing.

47. flowers in the breeze

_____

48. a shadow

_____

49. a cold draught

_____

50. the sun

_____

51. a gale

_____

52. a pencil sharpener

_____   /6

Write down a **noun** that can be made
from each **verb**, e.g. create = creation

53. examine _____ **54.** approve _____

55. enjoy _____ **56.** discover _____

57. medicate _____ **58.** deliver _____

59. extend _____ **60.** repeat _____   /8

Write two short definitions for each **homonym**.

61. ball   _____

62. ball   _____

63. fan   _____

64. fan   _____

65. tap   _____

66. tap   _____   /6

Unscramble these **anagrams** to find four types of fruit.

67. enpiplpea   _____

68. ftepgruair   _____

69. toparic   _____

70. aanabn   _____   /4

/70

PAPER 15

Storm

Grey blots stampede across the sky   1
angry elephants of water and air.
Gusts bellow and bully trees and roofs
Stealing timber and tiles,
while windows slapped by icy rain   5
teem with tears and whine in the wind.

Then power ebbing, the wind, retreating,
calls off clouds like errant guard dogs.
In their wake a sunburst victorious
lights up dripping branches   10
with a million fairy lights.

The storm is over.

Circle your answers.

1. Which object doesn't the poem say that the wind steals?

     timber   windows   tiles

2. Which of these animals is not mentioned in the poem?

     elephant   wolf   dog

3. How many fairy lights does the poem describe?

     a million   a thousand   millions

Answer these questions.

4. What does the word *stampede* (line 1) mean?

_____

5. What are the *angry elephants of water and air* (line 2)?

_____

6. Are the windows really crying? If not, what are the tears the poem describes?

_____

7. Write a sentence explaining how the mood in the first verse is different from that in the second.

_____

8–9. Find two examples of personification in the poem.

_____

_____

10. Find an example of simile in the poem.

_____

11. Find an example of alliteration.

_____

12. What are the fairy lights described in line 11?

_____   /12

> Write **abbreviations** for these.

13. Prime Minister _____

14. Royal Society for the Prevention of Cruelty to Animals _____

15. millimetres _____

16. World Wide Web _____

17. compact disc _____

18. January _____

19. New York _____

20. United Nations _____   /8

Write these sentences again with the correct punctuation.

21–33. Youll never believe what Ive just seen giggled Chloe

What asked Megan tell me quickly

_____

_____

_____

_____

_____ /13

Add a **suffix** to change each **noun** into a **verb**, e.g. standard = standardise.

34. vandal _____ **35.** pollen _____

36. class _____ **37.** vocal _____

38. apology _____ **39.** medic _____

40. note _____ /7

Write these sentences again, with the **subordinate clause** first.

41. My aunt fell ill when she was on holiday.

_____

42. We stood under the bridge until it stopped raining.

_____

43. We left the classroom quickly after the fire bell rang.

_____

44. I closed the rabbit's cage before it could escape.

_____

45. She put the light on so she could see where she was going.

_____

46. We decided to have the picnic although it was cloudy.

_____ /6

Write these words in alphabetical order, then add one word of your own to the beginning and end of the list.

> presume   presentable   president   pressure   prescription   preserve

47. _____   **48.** _____   **49.** _____

50. _____   **51.** _____   **52.** _____

53. _____   **54.** _____ /8

Add an **adjectival phrase** to complete each sentence.

55. The walls of the cave were streaming with _____ slime.

56. A _____ cloud covered the sun.

57. The dog left _____ across the cream carpet.

58. _____ blossom covered the trees.

59. A _____ smell wafted from the kitchen.

60. _____ bunting hung from the trees. /6

Move one letter from one word to the other, to make two new words.

61–62. crease   stain   _____   _____

63–64. grain   stem   _____   _____

65–66. bloat   patter   _____   _____ /6

Write two **definitions** for each word. One should be
a meaning that has come into use in recent years.

67–68. mouse _____

_____

69–70. notebook _____

_____

/4

/70

Glossary

abbreviation	a word that has been shortened, e.g. *hippo, UK*
abstract noun	a noun that names a feeling or idea, e.g. *happiness*
active verb	a verb where the subject of the sentence is the main focus, e.g *the man ate the apple*
adjectival phrase	a group of words that describe a **noun**
adjective	a word that describes a **noun**, e.g. *tiny, green*
adverb	a word that describes a **verb**, e.g. *kindly, prettily*
alliteration	creative writing technique where two or more words in a sentence begin with the same sound.
anagram	a word puzzle made by mixing up the letters in a word
antonym	a word with the opposite meaning to another word, e.g. *tall, short*
apostrophe	a **punctuation mark** used to show possession or **contraction**
clause	a part of a sentence that contains a **verb**
collective noun	a way of describing a group of a particular thing, e.g. *flock of sheep*
common noun	a word for an ordinary thing, e.g. *book, tree*
complex sentence	a sentence that contains a **main clause** and a **subordinate clause.**
compound word	a word made up of two other words, e.g. *footpath*
conditional clause	a **clause** in a sentence which describes how one thing depends on another. **If it is cold**, *I will wear a hat.*
conjunction	a word used to join parts of a sentence, e.g. *and, but, so*
connective	a word or words that join **clauses** or sentences
contraction	two words joined together, where an **apostrophe** marks letters that have been removed, e.g. *do not = don't*
definition	the meaning of a word
future tense	a verb tense that refers to something that will happen in the future
homonym	a word with the same spelling as another but a different meaning, e.g. *train*
homophone	a word which sounds the same but has a different spelling, e.g. *maid, made*
metaphor	where one thing is describes as being another, e.g. *He is a star.*

74

noun	a word that names a thing or person
object	the person or thing that the **verb** relates to in a sentence, e.g. *Lisa sang a* <u>*song*</u>.
onomatopoeia	a word that makes the sound that it describes, e.g. *bang*
passive verb	a **verb** where the object of the sentence is the focus, e.g. *The nut was eaten by the squirrel.*
past tense	a **verb** that describes something that has already happened
personification	where non-human things are described using human qualities, e.g. *The sun smiled on us*.
plural	more than one of something
prefix	a group of letters added to the beginning of a word to alter its meaning, e.g. *re, ex, co*
preposition	a word that describes the position of one thing in relation to another, e.g. *on, under, from*
present tense	a **verb** that describes what is happening now
pronoun	a word that can be used in the place of a **noun**
proper noun	the name of a person, place, day of the week, month of the year etc, e.g. *Jill, March, Rome*
proverb	a short memorable saying, e.g. *fortune favours the brave*
reported speech	what someone has said, without their actual words being used
root word	a word that **prefixes** or **suffixes** can be added to, to make new words
semi-colon	a punctuation mark used to separate **clauses** or phrases in a sentence.
simile	where one things is compared to another using the word as or like, e.g. *as old as the hills*
singular	just one of something
subject	who or what a sentence is about. e.g. <u>**Lisa**</u> *sang a song.*
suffix	a group of letters added to the end of a word to alter its meaning, e.g. *less, ful, ly*
synonym	a word with a similar meaning to another word, e.g. *large, huge*
verb	a doing or being word

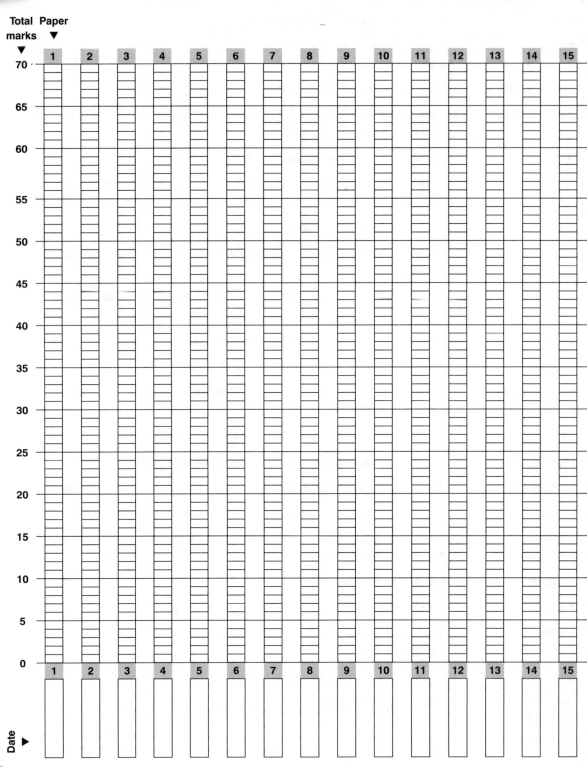

Total marks ▼ **Paper** ▼

| | 1 | 2 | 3 | 4 | 5 | 6 | 7 | 8 | 9 | 10 | 11 | 12 | 13 | 14 | 15 |

70
65
60
55
50
45
40
35
30
25
20
15
10
5
0

Date ▶

Now colour in your score!